MATH MASTERS: ANALYZE THIS!

Mixed Numbers

Claire Piddock

Educational Media

rourkeeducationalmedia.com

Scan for Related Titles and
Teacher Resources

Before Reading:

Building Academic Vocabulary and Background Knowledge

Before reading a book, it is important to tap into what your child or students already know about the topic. This will help them develop their vocabulary, increase their reading comprehension, and make connections across the curriculum.

1. Look at the cover of the book. What will this book be about?
2. What do you already know about the topic?
3. Let's study the Table of Contents. What will you learn about in the book's chapters?
4. What would you like to learn about this topic? Do you think you might learn about it from this book? Why or why not?
5. Use a reading journal to write about your knowledge of this topic. Record what you already know about the topic and what you hope to learn about the topic.
6. Read the book.
7. In your reading journal, record what you learned about the topic and your response to the book.
8. After reading the book complete the activities below.

Content Area Vocabulary

Read the list. What do these words mean?

common denominator
denominator
equivalent fraction
improper fraction
mixed number
multiple
number line
numerator
reciprocal

After Reading:

Comprehension and Extension Activity

After reading the book, work on the following questions with your child or students in order to check their level of reading comprehension and content mastery.

1. When denominators are not the same, how do you find a common denominator? (Summarize)
2. How can you use shapes to show wholes and parts of something? (Infer)
3. Can you label improper fractions on a number line? How? (Asking questions)
4. How do you convert a mixed number to an improper fraction? (Text to self connection)
5. What is a reciprocal and how do you find out what it is? (Asking questions)

Extension Activity

Practice all the concepts in the book to master mixed numbers!

Table of Contents

Mixed Number Models

Pizza Models

Are you hungry? Let's look at pizza models.

Whole:

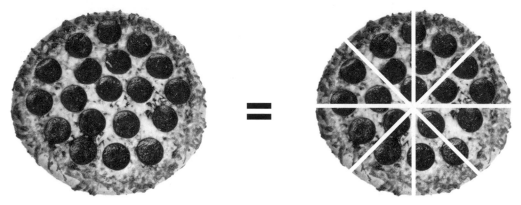

Here is a whole pizza, first uncut, then cut into 8 equal slices.

1 whole equals 8 of 8 equal parts or $\frac{8}{8}$.

Fraction:

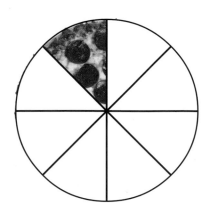

This slice is a fraction of the pizza. 1 part of 8 equal parts.

This fraction is $\frac{1}{8}$.

Put them together.
A **mixed number** has a whole number part
and a fraction part.

Mixed Number:

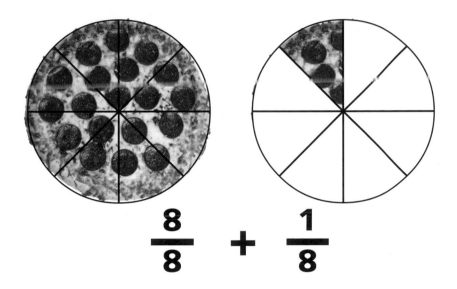

$$\frac{8}{8} + \frac{1}{8}$$

The whole pizza and $\frac{1}{8}$ of a pizza illustrate
the mixed number $1\frac{1}{8}$.

The top of a fraction is the
numerator. The bottom of a fraction
is the denominator.

$$\frac{4}{5} \quad \longleftarrow \bullet \text{ numerator}$$
$$\quad \longleftarrow \bullet \text{ denominator}$$

Shape Models

You can use other shapes to show wholes and parts.

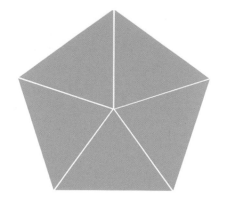

1 whole = $\frac{5}{5}$

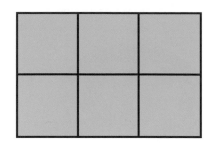

1 whole = $\frac{6}{6}$

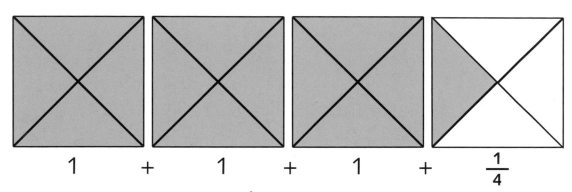

1   +   1   +   1   + $\frac{1}{4}$

The mixed number $3\frac{1}{4}$

1   + $\frac{2}{3}$

The mixed number $1\frac{2}{3}$

What mixed number does the model show?

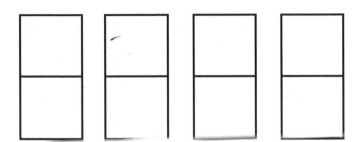

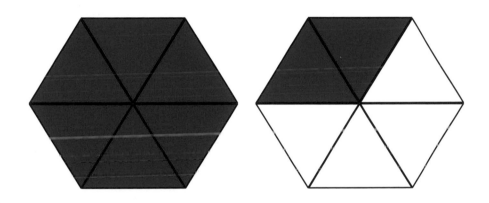

7

Number Lines

On a **number line** you can see how far away whole numbers and fractions are from 0.

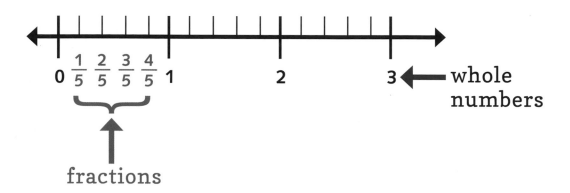

fractions

The tick marks between the whole numbers on the number line below represent mixed numbers.

This mixed number is $1\frac{2}{5}$ because it is $1\frac{2}{5}$ units to the right of 0.

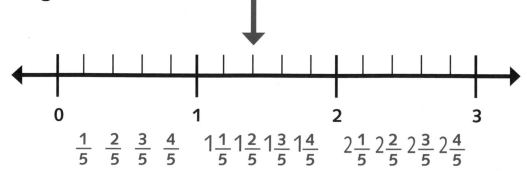

This number line is marked in thirds. Use the whole number distance from 0, and the number of thirds to the right of the whole number to name the points.

The mixed number at **A** is $1\frac{2}{3}$. The mixed number at **B** is $2\frac{1}{3}$.

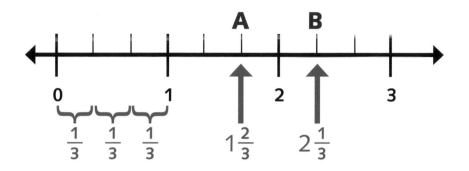

On what mixed number did the bug land?

a.

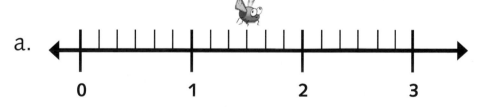

Answers:

a. $1\frac{3}{6}$

b. $2\frac{3}{4}$

c. $3\frac{7}{7}$

b.

c.

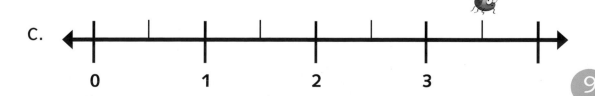

Mixed Numbers and Improper Fractions

Improper Fractions

You can label a fraction number line in a different way. Continue to label the fractions in fifths on this number line.

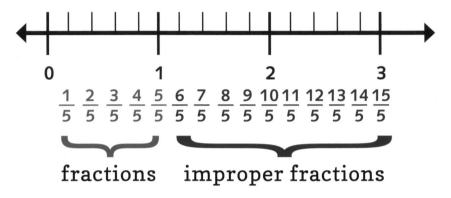

fractions   improper fractions

There is nothing wrong with improper fractions. They are just top heavy. An **improper fraction** is a fraction whose **numerator** is greater than its **denominator.**

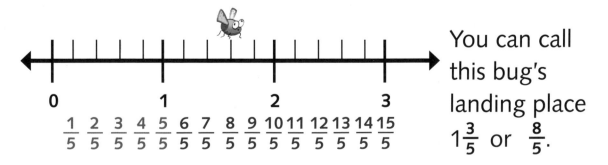

You can call this bug's landing place $1\frac{3}{5}$ or $\frac{8}{5}$.

They have the same value. They are equal. $1\frac{3}{5} = \frac{8}{5}$.

Remember…When the numerator and denominator are the same, the fraction equals 1.

Examples: $\frac{2}{2} = 1$ $\frac{3}{3} = 1$ $\frac{4}{4} = 1$ $\frac{5}{5} = 1$ $\frac{8}{8} = 1$

To write an improper fraction as a mixed number:

- Break up the improper fractions into as many 1s as possible.

$$\frac{8}{5} = \boxed{\frac{5}{5}} + \frac{3}{5}$$

$$\downarrow$$

- Then write the number of ones and the fraction that is left.

$$\frac{8}{5} = 1 + \frac{3}{5}$$

$$\frac{8}{5} = 1\frac{3}{5}$$

$$\frac{7}{3} = \boxed{\frac{3}{3}} + \boxed{\frac{3}{3}} + \frac{1}{3}$$

$$\downarrow \qquad \downarrow$$

$$\frac{7}{3} = 1 + 1 + \frac{1}{3} = 2 + \frac{1}{3}$$

$$\frac{7}{3} = 2\frac{1}{3}$$

You can use division to change an improper fraction to a mixed number. Divide the numerator by the denominator. Write the remainder as a fraction.

$$\frac{22}{5} \qquad 22 \div 5 = 4 \text{ remainder } 2 = 4\frac{2}{5}$$

To write a mixed number as an improper fraction:

- Write the whole number part as a sum of 1s.

$$3\frac{1}{4} = 1 + 1 + 1 + \frac{1}{4}$$

- Write each 1 as a fraction.

$$3\frac{1}{4} = \frac{4}{4} + \frac{4}{4} + \frac{4}{4} + \frac{1}{4}$$

- Add the numerators, and keep the denominator the same.

$$3\frac{1}{4} = \frac{4 + 4 + 4 + 1}{4}$$

$$3\frac{1}{4} = \frac{13}{4}$$

$$2\frac{5}{8} = 1 + 1 + \frac{5}{8}$$

$$2\frac{5}{8} = \frac{8}{8} + \frac{8}{8} + \frac{5}{8}$$

$$2\frac{5}{8} = \frac{8 + 8 + 5}{8}$$

$$2\frac{5}{8} = \frac{21}{8}$$

To **convert** a mixed number to an improper fraction or from a fraction to a mixed number is to change from one to the other.

What is $1\frac{2}{5}$ as an improper fraction?

What is $\frac{17}{4}$ as a mixed number?

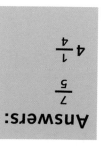

Add and Subtract Mixed Numbers

Add Mixed Numbers

To add mixed numbers with the same denominator, convert all numbers to improper fractions; then add.

$$2\frac{3}{5} + 1\frac{4}{5} = \frac{13}{5} + \frac{9}{5}$$

- Convert to improper fractions.

$$= \frac{13 + 9}{5} = \frac{22}{5}$$

- Add numerators. Keep the denominator.

$$= 4\frac{2}{5}$$

- Convert back to a mixed number.

The answer is $\frac{22}{5}$ as an improper fraction.

The answer is $4\frac{2}{5}$ as a mixed number.

Here is another way to add mixed numbers with like denominators.

$2\frac{3}{5} + 1\frac{4}{5}$

$2\frac{3}{5} + 1\frac{4}{5} = 2 + \frac{3}{5} + 1 + \frac{4}{5}$ • Add whole numbers.
Add fractions.
Then simplify.

$= 2 + 1 + \frac{3}{5} + \frac{4}{5}$ • Change the order of the addends.

$= 3 + \frac{3}{5} + \frac{4}{5}$ • Add the whole numbers.

$= 3 + \frac{3+4}{5} = 3 + \frac{7}{5}$ • Add the fractions.
Add numerators.
Keep the denominator the same.

$2\frac{3}{5} + 1\frac{4}{5} = 3 + 1\frac{2}{5}$ • Convert $\frac{7}{5}$ to a mixed number and add it to 3.

$= 4\frac{2}{5}$

The Commutative Property says that you can change the order of the addends without changing the sum.

$3 + 4 = 4 + 3$ $\qquad$ $\frac{2}{5} + \frac{1}{5} = \frac{1}{5} + \frac{2}{5}$

Subtract Mixed Numbers

To subtract mixed numbers with the same or like denominators.

Convert all numbers to improper fractions; then subtract.

$$3\frac{5}{8} - 1\frac{3}{8} = \frac{29}{8} - \frac{11}{8}$$

- Write each mixed number as an improper fraction.

$$= \frac{29 - 11}{8} = \frac{18}{8}$$

- Subtract the numerators. Keep the denominator the same.

$$= 2\frac{2}{8}$$

- Convert to a mixed number.

$$= 2\frac{1}{4}$$

- Simplify the fraction by dividing by the largest number that goes exactly into both 2 and 8.

$$\frac{2}{8} = \frac{2 \div 2}{8 \div 2} = \frac{1}{4}$$

When you simplify, you are finding an **equivalent fraction** with the smallest possible denominator. To find an equivalent fraction, multiply or divide numerator and denominator by the same number.

$$\frac{6}{10} = \frac{6 \div 2}{10 \div 2} = \frac{3}{5} \qquad \frac{3}{5} = \frac{3 \times 2}{5 \times 2} = \frac{6}{10}$$

Back to the pizza shop!

🍪 Suppose your team celebrates a win. There are $2\frac{3}{4}$ pizzas left on the table. The players are not done eating. They eat $1\frac{2}{4}$ pizzas more. How much pizza will be left?

🍪 The team spent $1\frac{2}{6}$ hours at the pizza shop and $\frac{5}{6}$ of an hour on the team bus to get home. How many hours did they spend on both activities?

17

Common Denominators

When the denominators are not the same, you need to find a **common denominator** in order to compute. Use equivalent fractions to make the denominators the same.

$$\frac{2}{3} \text{ and } \frac{1}{2}$$

- Denominators not the same.

$$\frac{2}{3} = \frac{2 \times 2}{3 \times 2} = \frac{4}{6}$$

- Multiply top and bottom of each fraction by the denominator of the other.

$$\frac{1}{2} = \frac{1 \times 3}{2 \times 3} = \frac{3}{6}$$

- Now both denominators are sixths!

Now you can add $1\frac{2}{3} + 3\frac{1}{2}$ using $1\frac{4}{6} + 3\frac{3}{6}$.

$$1\frac{2}{3} + 3\frac{1}{2} = 1\frac{4}{6} + 3\frac{3}{6}.$$

- Add whole numbers. Add fractions.

$$= 1 + 3 + \frac{4}{6} + \frac{3}{6}$$

- You can add in any order.

$$4 + \frac{7}{6} = 4 + 1 + \frac{1}{6}$$

- Simplify.

$$= 5\frac{1}{6}$$

If you walk your dog on a trail $2\frac{2}{3}$ miles long, and continue on a different trail $1\frac{1}{4}$ miles long, how far will you walk your dog?

It is important to label your answers with the correct unit or word, especially when the problem involves measurements, such as miles, inches, pounds, quarts, meters, liters, or kilograms.

Answer: $3\frac{11}{12}$ miles

Sometimes, one of the denominators is the common denominator.

If one denominator is a **multiple** of the other, use the larger denominator as the common denominator.

$\frac{3}{4}$ and $\frac{5}{8}$

- Multiples of 4 are 4, 8, 12, 16, and so on.

$\frac{3}{4}$ and $\frac{5}{8}$

- Denominators not the same, but you know 4 x 2 = 8.

$\frac{3}{4} = \frac{3 \times 2}{4 \times 2} = \frac{6}{8}$

- Multiply top and bottom of $\frac{3}{4}$ by 2. Now both denominators are eighths!

Now you can subtract $4\frac{3}{4} - 2\frac{5}{8}$ using $4\frac{6}{8} - 2\frac{5}{8}$.

$4\frac{3}{4} - 2\frac{5}{8} = 4\frac{6}{8} - 2\frac{5}{8}.$

$= \frac{38}{8} - \frac{21}{8}$

- Convert to improper fractions.

$= \frac{38 - 21}{8} = \frac{17}{8}$

- Subtract fractions.

$= 2\frac{1}{8}$

- Convert back to a mixed number.

$4\frac{3}{4} - 2\frac{5}{8} = 2\frac{1}{8}.$

If you were $52\frac{1}{8}$ inches tall last year, and you are $55\frac{1}{2}$ inches this year, how many inches did you grow?

21

Multiply with Mixed Numbers

$3 \times 1\frac{1}{2}$

Picture it.

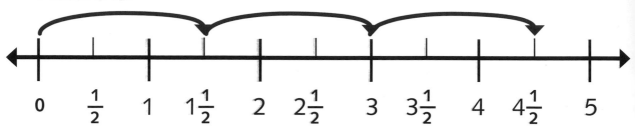

$$0 \quad \frac{1}{2} \quad 1 \quad 1\frac{1}{2} \quad 2 \quad 2\frac{1}{2} \quad 3 \quad 3\frac{1}{2} \quad 4 \quad 4\frac{1}{2} \quad 5$$

Three jumps of $1\frac{1}{2}$ land at $4\frac{1}{2}$ so, $3 \times 1\frac{1}{2} = 4\frac{1}{2}$.

Here's the calculation.

$3 \times 1\frac{1}{2}$

$\frac{3}{1} \times 1\frac{1}{2}$
- Write the whole number as a fraction with 1 in the denominator.

$\frac{3}{1} \times \frac{3}{2}$
- Write the mixed number as an improper fraction.

$\frac{3}{1} \times \frac{3}{2} = \frac{3 \times 3}{1 \times 2} = \frac{9}{2}$
- Multiply numerators. Multiply denominators.

$= 4\frac{1}{2}$
- Convert back to mixed number.

Every whole number can be written as a fraction with 1 in the denominator.

Examples:

$2 = \frac{2}{1}$ $3 = \frac{3}{1}$ $8 = \frac{8}{1}$ $12 = \frac{12}{1}$

You read a punch recipe that needs $3\frac{3}{4}$ cups of juice. How many cups of juice will you need if you make 4 times as much?

Answer:
15 cups

23

Divide with Mixed Numbers

You can also think of a fraction as the numerator divided by the denominator.

$\frac{2}{3}$ means 2 ÷ 3

2 loaves of bread divided into 3 pieces gives you 6 pieces…

that you share equally among 3 people

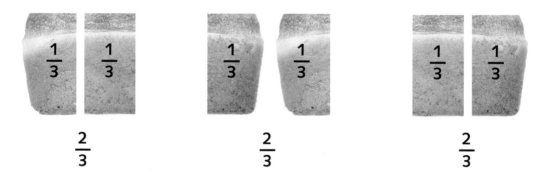

Each person gets $\frac{2}{3}$ of a loaf.

So 2 ÷ 3 has the same result as 2 x $\frac{1}{3}$.

$$\frac{3}{2} = 3 \div 2$$

3 loaves of bread divided into 2 pieces gives you 6 pieces…

that you share equally among 2 people

$1\frac{1}{2}$ $1\frac{1}{2}$

Each person gets 3 halves of a loaf.

$\frac{3}{2}$ or $1\frac{1}{2}$ loaves of bread.

So $3 \div 2$ has the same result as $3 \times \frac{1}{2}$.

Suppose you want to divide a 20-pound bag of potatoes into 8-pound bags. How many 8-pound bags of potatoes will you have?

Picture it. 20 pounds

Divide into 8-pound bags.

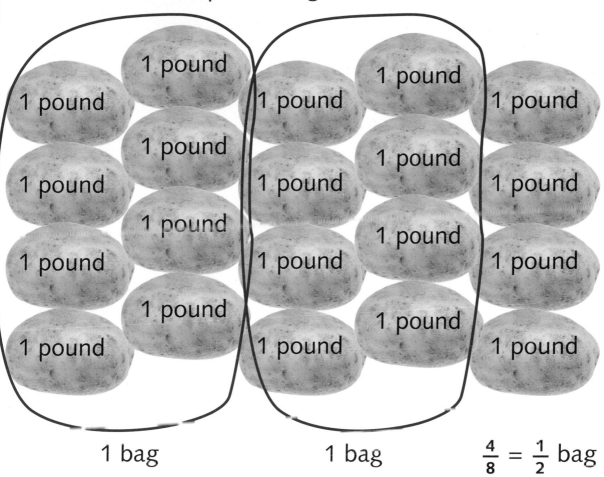

1 bag   1 bag $\frac{4}{8} = \frac{1}{2}$ bag

Here's the calculation.

$20 \div 8 = \frac{20}{8} = 2\frac{4}{8} = 2\frac{1}{2}$ bags

$20 \div 8$ has the same result as $20 \times \frac{1}{8}$

Suppose you have 19 pounds of potato chips to divide into 3 pound bags. How many bags of potato chips will you have?

Division of fractions and mixed numbers uses the **reciprocal** of a number. To get the reciprocal of a fraction, turn it upside down.

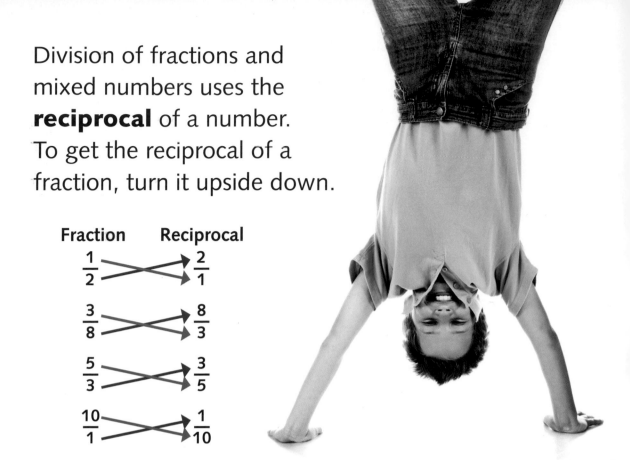

Fraction	Reciprocal
$\frac{1}{2}$	$\frac{2}{1}$
$\frac{3}{8}$	$\frac{8}{3}$
$\frac{5}{3}$	$\frac{3}{5}$
$\frac{10}{1}$	$\frac{1}{10}$

To divide by a mixed number, multiply by its reciprocal.

$$14 \div 2\frac{1}{3} = \frac{14}{1} \div 2\frac{1}{3}$$

• Write the whole number as a fraction.

$$= \frac{14}{1} \div \frac{7}{3}$$

• Write the mixed number as an improper fraction.

$$= \frac{14}{1} \times \frac{3}{7}$$

• Turn the improper fraction over to get its reciprocal. Then multiply.

$$= \frac{14 \times 3}{1 \times 7} = \frac{42}{7} = 6$$

The restaurant owner cuts a 10-foot long piece of fabric into pieces $1\frac{1}{4}$ feet long to make placemats. How many placemats will there be?

Glossary

common denominator (KAH-muhn di-NAH-muh-nay-tur): a denominator shared by several fractions

denominator (di-NAH-muh-nay-tur): in a fraction, the number that is below the line that shows how many equal parts the whole number can be divided into

equivalent fraction (i-QWIV-uh-luhnt FRAK-shuhn): a fraction that is equal to and can be used in place of another fraction

improper fraction (im-PRAH-pur FRAK-shuhn): a fraction whose numerator is greater than its denominator, as in $\frac{4}{3}$ or $\frac{15}{10}$

mixed number (mickst NUHM-bur): a number made up of a whole number and a fraction, such as $6\frac{1}{2}$

multiple (MUHL-tuh-puhl): a number that can be exactly divided by a smaller number

number line (NUHM-bur line): a line with equally spaced tick marks named by numbers to show how far away they are from 0

numerator (NOO-muh-ray-tur): in a fraction, the number above the line that shows how many parts of the denominator are taken

reciprocal (ri-SIP-ruh-kuhl): the reciprocal of a fraction is the fraction turned upside-down. For example, the reciprocal of $\frac{2}{3}$ is $\frac{3}{2}$

Index

Websites to Visit

www.commoncoresheets.com/SortedByGrade.php?Sorted=4nf3c

www.theproblemsite.com/printables/fraction-operations

www.worksheets.theteacherscorner.net/make-your-own/math-worksheets/basic-math/fractions-equations.php

About The Author

Claire Piddock lives by a pond in the woods of Maine with her husband and big dog, Otto. She loves painting landscapes, doing puzzles, and reading mysteries. She sees math as a fun puzzle and enjoys taking the mystery out of math as she has done for many years as a teacher and writer.

Meet The Author!
www.meetREMauthors.com

www.rourkeeducationalmedia.com

PHOTO CREDITS: Cover: numbers © brain/lightbulb © Positive Vectors, photo, circles © Vectors1; Page 4-5 pizza © Hurst Photo, page 5 © Matthew Cole; page 6 pentogram © ratselmeister; page 9 bug © Rocketsimages; page 17 © CattleyaArt; page 19 © Matthew Cole; page 21 © Veronica Louro; page 23 © Roslen Mack; page 24 © Igor Vkv; page 26 © roroto12p; page 28 © Be Good, page 29 © Elena Akinshina

Edited by: Keli Sipperley
Cover and Interior design by: Nicola Stratford   www.nicolastratford.com

Library of Congress PCN Data

Mixed Numbers / Claire Piddock
(Math Masters: Analyze This!)
ISBN 978-1-68191-733-7 (hard cover)
ISBN 978-1-68191-834-1 (soft cover)
ISBN 978-1-68191-927-0 (e-Book)
Library of Congress Control Number: 2016932657

Rourke Educational Media
Printed in the United States of America, North Mankato, Minnesota

Also Available as:
ROURKE'S
e-Books